TWELVE LINES

MUSKAAN KAKKAR

Made with ❤ on the Notion Press Platform
www.notionpress.com

To whomesoever is reading this:

I will not be paying for your therapy.

Contents

Contents

Contents

Foreword

Her ~

My journey with Muskaan began around five years ago. From the very first interaction, I noticed a spark of ebullience and a penchant for language that only served to grow over the years, in leaps and bounds.

Slowly, over my years of association with Muskaan, in the guise of a teacher, mentor and friend, I came to love watching her metamorphose into a prismatic lover of language and literature and especially of, poetry. She is, blessed with a bewitchingly melancholy soul of a poet. She is, carried by the power of her words and her ability to synthesize emotion with text. With pleasure, have I witnessed her blossom from a fledgling writer to a well of talent that you will enjoy reading today.

I am so proud of her for having taken the brave steps to write, compile and publish this remarkable first novel. This stellar achievement, I guarantee you, is supercharged with raw talent and I am so excited for you to witness her voice.

Dear Reader - As you turn the pages, I hope you lose yourself in her stellar writing. I promise you that this book is just the beginning of a long line of sanguine stories and song.

Immerse yourself and enjoy!

~ Amanda Conlan

Preface

You guys are going to skip this anyways so I can write whatever I want.

These poems are not just crafted words; they are fragments of a personal journey. They explore themes of vulnerability, resilience, and the ever-evolving search for meaning. As you read, I hope you'll find echoes of your own experiences, sparking introspection and igniting a sense of shared humanity.

The poems here don't shy away from the shadows. They delve into the darker corners of the heart, acknowledging the challenges and anxieties that weave themselves into the fabric of life. But alongside the shadows, you'll also find glimmers of hope, moments of joy, and the enduring strength of the human spirit.

Some poems may act as mirrors, reflecting emotions you recognize, experiences you've shared. Others might be windows, offering glimpses into worlds unseen, perspectives different from your own. Each poem is a shard of colored glass, contributing to the vibrant, ever-shifting image of what it means to be human.

Words are my tools, my paintbrush, and my chisel. I've sculpted them into metaphors and similes, crafted them into rhythmic stanzas, and woven them into narratives that paint vivid pictures in your mind. The beauty of language, its power to evoke emotions and transport you to different worlds.

This book is an invitation to a conversation, not a lecture. There are no definitive answers here, only questions whispered on the wind. The beauty of poetry lies in its ability to resonate with each reader in a unique way.

So, turn the page and embark on this journey of exploration. Let the words wash over you, ignite your imagination, and allow yourself to be unveiled, one verse at a time.

Aliferous

To be aliferous is to have wings. A student or a teenager DREAMS of a million things, from cracking highly competitive exams to earning millions. In our youth, we truly believe we have a pair of wings and we'll soar so high in the sky that we won't be able to see or face our problems on ground. This age is filled with excitement, new experiences, and adventure, along with failures, mistakes, and the crippling pressure of deciding your future or being suffocated in the future that is decided FOR YOU.

Teenage is more complex than just the academic stress. It is filled with insecurities, anxieties, and bullies; I can keep going. People have come to believe that somehow their worth will go through the roof if they just bring the other person's down to the ground. You don't know what battles people are fighting, so stay the hell out.

Having recently experienced this rollercoaster and coming near the end of my teenage years, I look back and contemplate what I could have done differently, and the answer is nothing. All the mistakes I made, the wrong decisions I took, I didn't know any better. Only if they asked what I want to do with my life, a little later in life.

1. I'm Too Young For This

I'm too young for this
To spend my nights worrying rather than a sound sleep
Every second I waste, there's an opportunity that I miss
Like my life will take turns if I god forbid, oversleep
Why are my seventeen year old shoulders burdened with the weight of my future?
Life went from cartoon to carbon, god has a sense of humor
Can't we decide how my entire life will pan out
After I've actually known what's it all about
Competition is cut throat, everybody needs that degree
But if this is how it is then I will fight, fight with everything that's left in me
I will embrace this part of my life and I will take the hits
But still nobody told me when I began, that I'm too young for this

2. Mirror, Mirror On The Wall

Mirror mirror on the wall
She's yet again stuck in a brawl
Whether she's worth it or not
It was her self esteem that took the shot
Was that joke absolutely necessary?
Damage was permanent, the laugh temporary
All she wants is respect you can very well tell
The bar is so low it's a tripping hazard in hell
So mirror mirror on the wall
Tell her to stand tall
Whether they fire bullets or comments
She did nothing to deserve that torment

3. Jack of All Trades

There are so many things out there,
Waiting to be tried
So, drop all your despair
And let skills and opportunity coincide
Go through hell and still thrive.
Let them know you're still persisting,
Or let me ask you, are you alive,
Or just existing?
Never be afraid of the undone,
Trust in what you've begun.
For, a jack of all trades is a master of none
But often better than a master of one.

4. Time Will Tell

It moves slowly when you wait,

Faster in joy,

You'll soon be standing on the gate,

Of the dreams you're about to conquer or destroy

You must know what it is by now

As it is the healer and the killer

Time has always won

And each time with great vigor

Let it heal your wounds

And let it take away your sufferings,

For you and I both want the moon,

But are we ready for the beginning?

5. Rule of The Jungle

There's no place for the weak here
The world is a jungle which we've constructed
And there's one rule dear
Either hunt or be hunted
Some of us still believe in redemption
But let's be honest
Humanity is far from that exception
So why pretend to be modest?
Survive for yourself
Fight for the chair
Because
Who said life is fair?

6. I'd Kill Regret First

I wanna start something new

But the past experiences keep me away

Regret oh regret when will I be free of you

Can't you let me breathe for a day?

My hands quiver as I try something I've failed at before

My heart beats faster than my brain can count

There's always a sense of doubt therefore

I am missing out on things and on whose account?

My bones are strained from the weight of the lives I could've lived

The fate's twisted, luck is cursed

Every chance it got it has revived

If murder was legal, I'd kill regret first

Wrath

Not to be dramatic or anything with the title. Being hurt by someone you trust feels like a violation of the soul. It's a visceral experience, a gut punch that leaves you gasping for air. Imagine a metaphorical surgeon, wielding scalpels of betrayal, meticulously dissecting your very being. That's the kind of pain we're talking about here. The initial reaction? It's natural to want payback. An eye for an eye, a primal scream for every tear. Vengeance might dance in your head, a twisted fantasy of making them feel the same gut-wrenching agony they inflicted. But here's the sobering truth: that is neither ideal nor possible.

Learning to control that rage and not let it cloud your judgement so you don't end up with your fingers on a trigger is a skill. A skill unfortunately I haven't mastered yet, so I WRITE. I write about those strong, overwhelming feelings and things I would do if murder were legal. Whatever you do, don't let your feelings and emotions rule your actions because feelings change very quickly, but actions are never forgiven or forgotten with the same speed.

7. I'll Watch You Burn

I'm over it
But I didn't deserve it
The look in your eyes when you betrayed
The one person who stayed
The warmth I felt around you
Would freeze me soon I knew
Now all they remember is the pain
I'd rather lose my hands than hold yours again
The silence I heard with my head to your chest
Often interrupted by your heart beats
Was deafening enough at best
For a bastard who cheats
My forgiveness won't get you anywhere
Soon enough the tables will turn
You'll pay for what you did here
Or in hell, I'll watch you burn

8. Dagger in My Back

You enjoy talking shit about me
Maybe that's all you're capable of
Narrating stories upon which only you agree
Tell me, was my respect easy to shove?
You can leave now, from this friendship you are free
Things I am mad about? Honey, I've lost track
Because you were supposed to fight the battle with me
But on the battleground, you stuck a dagger in my back
Life is unfair but I trust karma's balance
Call me a bitch, I'll take that respect, but
I would rather adjust my life to your absence
than adjust my boundaries to tolerate your disrespect

9. Liar

"Liar liar pants on fire"
We would say if we were still eight
But you never grew any higher
And that's clear by your moral compass' state
I can forgive your deed but the lying?
Trust is what any relation is built on
You won't win it back, you can die trying
This is isn't something even worth fighting upon
Could've been honest, would that have cost you a lot?
You've woven a web of lies, and you'll be the one caught
I intend on telling you the truth, a courage you lack
Just as soon as I'm done stitching the wounds your lies made
on my back

10. Dead to Me

Saw you after ages today
More like a silhouette of someone I adored
More than your words, your actions conveyed
Didn't even flinch when you ripped the cord
Your eyes meet mine and as much as I try to care
You're dead to me, I hope you are aware
After you made them drown in tears of pain
There's still some dignity I've got to maintain
It's funny how time changes the perspective
Of someone's existence, now ineffective
Trust me, I mean it when I say, I used to love you
But now I wouldn't care if a bus hit you

11. Acrimony

Where there is anger
There is pain underneath
Something is our anchor
And is dropped way beneath
It stems from different places
I didn't know existed in my head
Sometimes can't see some faces
Without imagining them dead
We might have different reasons
To keep that anger underneath
I say never tame your demons
But always keep 'em on a leash.

12. You Killed Something

Look in her eyes, you killed something

The glimmer of hope that could make you believe even in a dumb thing

Once where there was an ocean of dreams and ambitions

Is now a pool of tears that are shed in the night while changing positions

She hangs on to her last piece of strength, still stronger than most around her

The grip is hurting her, I hope your reasons were worth it, whatever they were

Where you could once tell her entire story in a glance

Today there is just a pair of eyes in a state of a trance

She watched it fall apart, she'll build it back up, always on her own

You were never a part of her story, she's in it all alone

Whatever you did, I hope it wasn't all for nothing

Because look in her eyes, you killed something

13. Pain is Red

Do you know what pain is?
Well, let me paint you a picture
Pain is when you hold back a tear and struggle to the end of
the sentence
Your eyes are drowning with vengeance
Pain is what your heart feels when you lose something dear
No medicine can heal a wound so severe
Pain is when you happily twist the knife, destroying your
insides
Just because they were once full of butterflies for the one
holding the knife
Pain is what pierces through you
When you hear that one sentence that holds the power to
crumble you
The picture is almost done, my paint is dried out
Did my hand fumble or was it red throughout?

5 feet of chaos

Just for context, I am 5 feet (5'1 but okay). This next part comprises poems written on a very personal level. It is said adversity doesn't build character; it reveals it. I happen to think that revelation can be seen in one's eyes. The eyes, as they say, are truly windows to the soul. There's a unique way our gaze transforms when emotions are raw and unfiltered. When genuine emotions are present, there's a subtle shift in our gaze that can be incredibly telling. It's a reminder that nonverbal communication is a powerful tool, and learning to read the language of the eyes can offer valuable insights into the hearts and minds of those around us. Try maintaining eye contact with a liar, a manipulator, a person who loves you and the one you love and notice the difference.

But for that to happen, you have to be true to yourself. Be comfortable in your skin, as they say. You are who you are. Try to be better obviously, but don't hate the current version either. Forging a personality that is meant to be liked by others will only push your true one so deep down that it will start corroding your insides. How long do you think you'll be able to keep up the facade? It's always better to showcase your true self and attract people because you'll always know they love YOU for YOU.

14. Brown Eyes

I have brown eyes
But they are so much more than dusky
They speak first whenever I'm caught in lies
They hold secrets deeper than the sea
I have brown eyes
They represent the strength of my soul
Wearing no disguise,
They tell the story as a whole
I have brown eyes
Stare long enough, sets your soul on fire
But you can see a part of me dies,
Whenever my eyes are called a liar.

15. See it in My Eyes

Can't you see it in my eyes?
How they sparkle when I spot you in a crowd
Or how they long for you when you're not around
Can't take them off, lord save them from what they've found
I've come so close to telling you about the storm brewing in my brain
Stopped myself because there's a friendship I've got to maintain
I fear we'll stay silent and the moment will pass
And 20 years later we'll just be someone in each other's class
It's new, it's risky but anything worth having involves a leap of faith
I'll jump again and again if that's what it takes
Everytime I see you, a part of me dies
And you idiot, you still can't see it in my eyes

16. Egomaniac

I am narcissistic

Not the cocky, manipulative kind

But in this world full of pessimistic

I am appalled by my own mind

I don't care if the world sees it as a negative trait

Lord knows its difficult to be sedate

I am brave enough to adore every flaw

That was given when something was seized from my claw

So go ahead and judge me for my sinful deeds

Find me guilty on what charges, pray tell?

I protect a narrative no one needs

I'll stand by myself even if it's a cold day in hell.

17. The Girl I Used to Be

The girl I used to be was afraid
Afraid of what people thought about her
Afraid of what could go wrong with her
Afraid that her lines were blurred
The girl I used to be was quiet
Quiet about what she truly felt
Quiet about what was going on in her head
Quiet about all the time she knelt
The girl I used to be was worried
Worried about her future
Worried about her past
Worried that life was passing her too fast
I'm no longer the girl I used to be
I'm strong, powerful, and brave
I'm ambitious and victorious
I'm no longer anyone's slave
I'll forever be grateful
But I'll never look back
I'll keep my lessons, from
The girl I used to be.

18. Do You Believe in Magic?

Do you believe in magic? I do
Not in moving things with my head but moving people with
my words
The smile I see on someone's face when they feel appreciated
Somehow holds the power to make a horrible day alleviated
Whether it's complimenting their smile or their soul
When you mention their strengths, you heal a hole
Of their insecurities, they constantly overthink about
Little do they know, they are beautiful inside and out
Barely takes a few seconds to pay a compliment
They might be struggling and you just threw them a life boat
and went
A giant ball of ego and stubbornness would break with one
word
So believe me when I tell you, magic always did exist

19. Blood is Thicker Than Water?

Blood is thicker than water, they say

But it becomes false when you meet people along the way

They are not related by blood but by loyalty

Because they were still here when life showed you her cruelty

They've seen me at my worst, at my best

They've seen me have a breakdown or ace a test

Whether I need a pen or a shoulder to cry on

I knew they will come through for me no matter what of their own they have going on

From stressing over formulae to college admissions

We've seen each other work so hard for our ambitions

They are so important to me because when life breaks you apart

They are right there willing to mend your heart

20. Whispers in the mirror

A mirror's reflection, a distorted display,
Imperfections magnified, stealing the day.
Worth measured by others, a like or a share,
A hollow comparison, a burden to bear.
The whispers of "not enough," a constant refrain,
Achievements belittled, washed clean by the rain.
Success of another, a personal sting,
Dimming the light, the joy it could bring.
Embrace the imperfections, the cracks in the shell,
For beauty resides where authenticity dwells.
Let go of comparisons, a path that deceives,
Focus on growth, on the strength that believes.
The journey is long, with stumbles and falls,
But courage persists, through echoing calls.
For insecurities lessen, with each step you take,
Shine your true light, for your own sake.

Paint me a picture

Narrative poetry, a marriage of storytelling and verse, weaves a tapestry of words that transports us through time and space. It is a potent blend of plot, character, and language, captivating readers with its rhythmic pulse and the unfolding drama within its lines.

Furthermore, narrative poetry thrives on the creation of vivid characters. Through descriptive language and dialogue, poets breathe life into their creations. We meet heroes facing daunting challenges, villains consumed by darkness, and flawed individuals grappling with their inner demons.

For writers, crafting a narrative poem requires a unique blend of skills. We must not only be adept at storytelling but also possess a strong command of language and poetic techniques. The ability to condense a story into verse while maintaining narrative tension and emotional resonance is a true mark of a skilled narrative poet.

In conclusion, narrative poetry is more than just a collection of verses. It is a symphony of story, character, and language, transporting us to different worlds and enriching our understanding of the human experience. Its ability to connect us to both the past and the present, to heroes and villains, to grand emotions and subtle nuances, ensures its enduring place in the literary world.

As long as there are stories to tell and emotions to evoke, narrative poetry will continue to captivate readers and inspire writers for generations to come.

21. The Tea

A beautiful summer afternoon it was

Mr. Vizak loved to sip his tea outside because

Life was treating him harshly, he said

Not for long, cause that eve they found Mr. Vizak dead

Panic in the country house, everybody a suspect

Heart attack, that's what the autopsy reflect

The house mourned Mr. Vizak, gone too soon

And the house was back in order, on a beautiful summer afternoon

Mrs. Vizak sat in her rocking chair

Reminiscing Mr. Vizak and his affair

Or how she'd end up with a broken limb

Because life was too harsh on him

She sat and starred at the beautiful scenery

Sipping, wondering how life would vary

Now that Mr. Vizak is six feet below

The tea was her doing, but no one would know

22. The House We Knew About

There was this house we knew about
After all we played nearby
But the holiness of it was in doubt
And no one could deny
We made up stories about what lay inside
The four walls contained a strong force
Was it someone who died?
And filled the house with remorse?
Night by night, it proliferated
Shivers down the backbone
And everything we thought we saw obliterated
As the ghosts were our own

23. The Devil's Favourite

The wings of an angel are faith and hope
The wings of the devil look rather red,
The legends run around the globe
They are anything but dead
Be careful, the devil has a pretty face
Think about it, it's not a race
Fools rush in where angels fear to tread
You can grow back whatever you have shed
You are born with angels on your side, savor it
For all you know
You may grow up to be the
Devil's favourite.

24. The Oak Tree

On a beautiful tree, on a beautiful afternoon, a bird forged a
nest she'd call home
The leaves of the tree moving delicately with the breeze while
for food the bird would roam
The leaves kept the young bird entertained
Her mother would find her moving in glee with them, her
happiness, unexplained
Soon the young bird fell sick, poisoned it may seem
The mother grew worried, doing whatever it takes to redeem
She ate the food she brought before her daughter did
She believed an outsider was poisoning her kid
She soon learnt that the tree she called home was an oak
Known to be poisonous to birds, her heart broke
Now the young one was as gone as the mother's will to live
Should she mourn her kid or the fact that she lived?

25. The Mighty King

The king, a mountain carved from weathered stone
Throned where the sun dipped low, a fiery crown
His beard, a silver river, tumbling down
Across his chest, where armor, etched and known
Gleamed like a mirrored ocean in the hall.
His voice, a rolling thunder, shook the wall
Commanding silence, eyes like molten gold,
A gaze that pierced through hearts, both young and old.
He spoke of battles won on distant shores,
Of empires conquered, kneeling at his door.
His laughter boomed, a storm across the land
A mighty king, with power in his hand.

26. The Flame

The flame, a twisting dancer, light and sly,
From humble spark to hungering, golden eye.
It licks and curls, a hungry, dancing tongue,
On kindling dry, a hungry song is sung.
Fire we hold, with reverence and fear,
A force of change, both beautiful and clear.
It lights our way, and brings the world to dust,
A primal power, a whisper we can't trust.
But embers fade, the dance begins to slow,
A dying gasp, a crimson afterglow.
The ash remains, a silent, fragile trace,
A memory of fire's fierce and fleeting grace.

Derision

Derision, the act of mocking and belittling someone or something, is a powerful weapon wielded in the social arena. But here in this context, this next section contains poems with satire. Satire, a literary device that uses humor, irony, exaggeration, or sarcasm to criticize something. It holds up a funhouse mirror to society, politics, or human nature, reflecting our flaws in a distorted but recognizable way. By laughing at these distortions, satire aims to make us think critically about the issues it targets. It can be a powerful tool for social change, prompting us to question the status quo and work towards a better world.

One of satire's key strengths is its ability to bypass defenses. Unlike a direct attack, its witty barbs disarm and engage the audience. We laugh at the absurdity of the situation, only to realize, with a startled jolt, that the absurdity is rooted in reality. Political cartoons skewering corruption, for example, use humor to make unpalatable truths more palatable.

However, satire is a double-edged sword. Its effectiveness relies heavily on context and audience. A joke that lands perfectly for one group might be lost or offensive to another. Additionally, satire can be misinterpreted as simple mockery, missing its deeper message.

In conclusion, satire is a powerful tool that uses humor to illuminate societal flaws and injustices. It can be a catalyst for change, prompting reflection and sparking healthy debate. While its effectiveness depends on context and audience, satire's ability to both entertain and critique makes it a vital force in a functioning society. Laughter, after all, can be a powerful weapon, reminding us that even the most serious issues can sometimes be addressed with a well-placed satirical jab.

27. Opinions, Strictly Limited

Since chivalry's a myth, and equality's a bore,
Behold the handbook for men, a guide to evermore!
Women, fragile creatures, built of porcelain and lace,
Need a firm hand to guide them, to set them in their place.
Their domain, the kitchen, a haven of flour,
Where they whip up our meals, by the clock and the hour.
For logic and reason, they simply can't cope,
Leave the thinking to the men, while they tend to the soap.
Keep her on a leash, but make it seem sweet,
Decisions are yours, hers are for the home committee.
A gentle suggestion, a leading remark,
Ensure she follows your path, right down to the park.
(But between you and me, and the stars in the sky,
These notions are outdated, a ridiculous lie.
For women are strong, with minds sharp and keen,
And a world that ignores them, will surely convene,
This handbook, of course, is a blatant farce,
A satire on outdated views, a societal scar.)

28. The Influential One

In the realm of endless scrolling, where attention spans are thin,

Vacations galore, on beaches pristine,

(Ignoring the sponsored posts, the deals in between).

Designer this, designer that, a life so grand,

(Ignoring the mountains of debt, the credit card in hand).

A fleeting high that fuels the fire, through day and endless night.

For every heart and thumbs-up, a validation's gentle hum,

A metric of their worthiness, a victory they've won.

But beneath the filtered surface, a hollowness resides,

A yearning for connection, that the digital world hides.

For real conversations falter, replaced by emojis bright,

And genuine emotions struggle, lost in the artificial light.

So next time you see a selfie, with a caption oh so deep,

Remember, it's all a show, a world where fakery can sleep.

Find joy in real connections, in laughter and in tears,

Not in the validation of strangers, and the echo of their cheers.

29. The Ballad of the Bribe

In bureaucracies bloated, where paperwork piles high,

Lives a creature most cunning, with a sly, knowing eye.

It slithers and whispers, with a smile oh so sweet,

Corruption's the name, and its methods can't be beat.

The media, with spotlights, exposes the game,

But outrage is fleeting, a flickering flame.

A public outcry, a promise to mend,

But the cycle continues, with no real end.

So raise a glass high, to the art of the bribe,

Where morals are flexible, and honesty can't survive.

Let's hope for a future, where truth takes its stand,

And corruption gets buried, beneath a righteous hand

30. Anxiety's grip

He'd wake in a panic, with sweat on his brow,
Convinced of a meteor, or a zombie cow.
The toaster would spark, a fire ignite,
His mind conjuring visions, of a world burning bright.
Public speaking? A nightmare untold,
His palms slick with terror, his voice weak and cold.
Every email a threat, every phone call a fright,
His fight-or-flight instincts, on constant high flight.
A symptom he'd diagnose, with a web search in hand,
Each article a rabbit hole, in the digital sand.
"Is this lump a tumor? Am I doomed to expire?"
Dr. Google's pronouncements, setting his soul on fire.
But sometimes, a moment, of clarity'd break,
A realization dawning, for goodness sake!
That most of his worries, were phantoms of dread,
And a little perspective, could calm his head instead.

31. The Chameleon Charmer

Belinda of Bending, a pleaser so keen,
A human pretzel, a never-ending scene.
She'd twist and she'd turn, a chameleon's art,
Reflecting desires, to win every heart.
Her smile, ever-present, a sunshine facade,
Ignoring her feelings, a truth never had.
"Of course, I agree!" her mantra so bright,
Ignoring her wishes, extinguished from sight.
But whisper a question, of her own hidden fire,
And Belinda might crumble, her facade start to tire.
For true connection, lies in authenticity's embrace,
Not a shape-shifting shadow, in a happiness chase.
So next time you see Belinda, with her smile oh-so-sweet,
Remember, true friendships can't be beat.
Speak your own truth, let your desires take flight,
For happiness blossoms, in the honest, full light.

32. Dream Designer's Deceit

In slumber's soft clutches, where reason takes flight,
Dreams unfurl, a kaleidoscope, both absurd and so bright.
We chase singing squirrels, through fields of blue cheese,
While logic vacations, replaced by surreal ease.
Last night, I was royalty, with a crown made of cheese,
My loyal corgi subjects, all barking with glee.
We fought off a dragon, who breathed fireflies bold,
And conquered the kingdom, with stories untold.
Dreams promise solutions, to life's tangled mess,
The winning lottery numbers, a financial success.
We wake up with hope, then a sigh of despair,
The reality bites, that the numbers weren't there.
So next time you dream, of adventures untold,
Remember don't let them take hold.
They're a playground for fancy, a whimsical flight,
Enjoy the absurdity, and greet the morning's light.

7 SINS

Sounds ominous I know. The concept of the seven sins, also known as the deadly sins, has transcended religious doctrine to become a universal language for understanding human flaws. These seven sins – pride, greed, wrath, envy, sloth, lust, and gluttony – represent fundamental desires and emotions that, when taken to an extreme, can lead to destructive behavior.

While these sins represent the pitfalls of human nature, they are not a condemnation. Recognizing these tendencies within ourselves serves as a starting point for self-improvement.

The seven deadly sins are not meant to be a source of shame, but rather a tool for self-reflection. By understanding these internal forces, we can strive for moderation and balance. The journey towards virtue lies in recognizing our shortcomings and actively working to cultivate positive qualities like humility, generosity, self-control, contentment, and temperance.

While the concept of the seven sins may have originated in a religious context, their relevance extends far beyond. They serve as a universal language, reminding us of the pitfalls that lie on the path of life. By navigating these internal obstacles, we can strive to become better individuals and contribute to a more harmonious society.

33. Pride

With peacock's strut and haughty chin, I reign,
The primal sin, of self-inflicted pain.
Pride, they call me, a serpent in disguise,
With whispered flattery, I taint and hypnotize.
My venom flows, in grand achievements told,
Of victories won, and stories to be bold.
I blind the mind to flaws and errors made,
In self-worship's mirror, a flawless image displayed.
Love's embrace, I turn to ash and dust,
For equal footing, pride harbors no trust.
Relationships crumble, with walls I construct,
A lonely kingdom, with affection defunct.
For pride builds a wall, where empathy ends,
A solitary throne, where no love transcends.
The fall from its peak, a humbling sight,
A shattered illusion, bathed in cold light.

34. Greed

They call me Greed, a serpent in disguise,
With eyes that hunger, and a heart that lies.
I crave the glitter, the endless delight,
More jewels, more riches, to fill up the night.
I whisper of power, a throne built of gold,
Of mansions and yachts, stories yet untold.
Contentment's a stranger, a concept so frail,
There's always a void, a hunger that trails.
Friendships I measure, in worth and in gain,
The loyalty bought, leaves a bitter stain.
Love is a weakness, a burden to bear,
Unless it brings profit, a treasure to share.
Beware of my whispers, the hunger that calls,
True happiness lies not in gilded walls.
For love and connection, are treasures untold,
More precious than diamonds, or riches of old.

35. Wrath

A fire I am, in the heart's deepest core,
A rage ever burning, a tempest that roars.
They call me by name, a whisper, a shout,
Wrath, the destroyer, what tears hope out.
A slight, a misunderstanding, a spark in the night,
Ignites my fury, a blinding white light.
Reason extinguished, by anger's fierce hold,
Words turn to weapons, stories untold.
Vengeance I crave, a score I must settle,
Leaving behind ashes, a heart full of mettle.
Broken bridges, trust turned to ash,
The weight of this burden, a terrible crash.
Beware of my whispers, the fire's hot breath,
True strength lies in forgiveness, that conquers death.
Let go of the embers, the anger release,
Find solace in calmness, and inner peace.

36. Envy

A serpent of shadows, where sunlight won't reach,
I slither and coil, with a bitter speech.
They call me by name, a whisper so sly,
Envy, the thief, with a tearful, wet eye.
I steal all your joys, and twist them in sight,
Turning sunshine to darkness, with all of my might.
Merit diminishes, achievements unseen,
Consumed by the poison, this venomous green.
I whisper in darkness, comparisons made,
Building a prison, of self-pity's shade.
Friendship withers, trust withers away,
Lost in the shadows, where envy holds sway.
Let go of the poison, the comparisons cease,
Embrace your own journey, find inner release.
For blessings abound, if you open your eyes,
Unique is your path, beneath sunlit skies.

37. Sloth

In slumber I dwell, in a fog soft and deep,
Apathy's blanket, where worries all sleep.
They call me Sloth, a whisper so slow,
A master of stalling, with nowhere to go.
Tasks pile up high, like mountains of sand,
The weight of tomorrow, a burden unplanned.
"Later," I murmur, a sigh and a yawn,
Motivation extinguished, a battle long gone.
Opportunities vanish, like smoke in the breeze,
While others find purpose, and climb life's tall trees.
Regret is a serpent, that coils in my chest,
A wasted existence, where dreams find no rest.
Beware of my whispers, the comfort's embrace,
True joy lies in striving, in leaving your space.
Set goals and pursue them, with passion alight,
For a life filled with purpose, burns ever so bright.

38. Lust

A flicker of flame, a yearning so deep,
In shadows I lurk, where desires I keep.
They call me by name, a whisper, a sigh,
Lust, the deceiver, with a tempting eye.
A touch, a caress, a glance that ignites,
A hunger for pleasure, that burns ever bright.
Reason surrenders, to passion's decree,
A reckless pursuit, of what I can't see.
Blind to the heart, to the soul's gentle plea,
Lost in the moment, a wild ecstasy.
Promises whispered, like smoke in the air,
Leaving behind ashes, and nothing to share.
Beware of my whispers, the fire's hot breath,
True love's a journey, not a moment of death.
Seek connection that lingers, a warmth that remains,
Where respect and compassion, ease life's bitter strains.

39. Gluttony

I call myself Pleasure, a name that beguiles,
But gluttony's hunger, behind my smile hides.
A bottomless well, where desire takes hold,
A never-ending feast, a story untold.
The table's a battlefield, senses ignite,
A symphony of flavors, a glorious sight.
Sweetness and spice, a decadent blend,
Reason surrenders, to this hedonistic end.
Health fades away, a forgotten decree,
Mobility lessens, a prisoner I see.
The joy of the table, a burden it grows,
Isolation sets in, as my spirit decomposes.
Beware of my whispers, the comfort they bring,
True pleasure's a balance, a harmonious spring.
Nourish your body, with mindful delight,
Savor each morsel, and find inner light.

Find Yourself

The 39 poems you just read were all created with empathy, endurance, wisdom, creativity, and a wealth of literary methods. In addition to expressing myself, my intention was to inspire others to write. The next pages are for you to try your hand at writing for the same purpose. Right and wrong are nonexistent, as are rules. After finishing this book, write a poem, a narrative, or just your thoughts. Since it's YOUR area, YOU get to design every element of it.

Just in case you need any help, there's a question on every page that needs answering.

Aliferous

Write about the struggles you faced as a teenager, the insecurities, the pressure, everything.

Wrath

Wrath consumes you, how do you plan to avoid that?

5 Feet Of Chaos

Tell me about a time when you realised something by someone's eyes.

Paint Me A Picture

Try telling a story in twelve lines.

Derision

Tell me a harsh truth but make it funny but not offensive.

7 Sins

Evil or necessary evil?